CRⵁP CIR

2017

Extraterrestrial Knowledge

ANDREW G FREW

Contents

Dedication

This book is dedicated to Lucy a four year old who gave us a different perspective on the shapes in the Crop Circles by naming them. Also I have felt deep inside while interpreting Crop Circles that I am not being taught by alien adults but by the alien children. Since, the future belongs to our children this book is so, dedicated.

Note from Author

Like most people I have never really paid much attention to Crop Circles, they have just seemed to me to be harmless phenomena that the farmers of the fields were singularly annoyed about. The kind of groups that gathered around these Crop Circles seemed to me to be the New Age types, who advocated a new way of living. At first these Crop Circle designs were just circles, hence the name they have been given and they all just seemed perpetrated, after all anybody could make a circle in a field and claim it made by aliens! I was very skeptical of Crop Circles and when news reports broke that they were claimed to be made by men as a UFO hoax I left the whole idea of any serious study of them in the proverbial bin. But since those early days of Crop Circle formations, thirty years ago, I have witnessed a gradual complexity in them that has stunned the imagination to such an extent of concluding that these geometrical patterns are so complex humans have not that ability to make them. I was left with an enigma, what do they mean, what are they telling us, is any language used or knowledge contained within them. This book is the result of my research into Crop Circles and my finding.

Introduction

In this work we are going to explore the hidden knowledge behind Crop Circles indeed the greatest phenomenon of the millennia. I have taken all the documented sightings of Crop Circles archived from the year 2017 and analysed their meaning giving a photo as it appeared alongside a graphic detail and a cosmic presentation of the knowledge contained within the message from the Crop Circle. It is for the reader to decide whether my analysis is correct. I know there are skeptics to this phenomenon who believe this is a human prank, but for my study I have only included Crop Circles that are considered genuine. This process is done by studying the broken stems of the plant. It has been found those stem nodes that have undergone internal combustion are a sure sign of a genuine made natural Crop Circle without human contamination. Below is given the examination of the plant within the Crop Circle after formation.

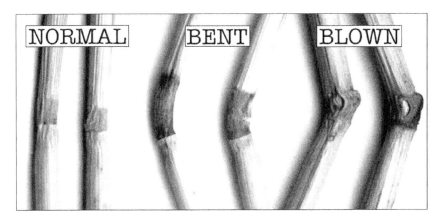

The normal, how the plant appears, the bent due to human activity and the blown, the sign that a genuine Crop Circle has formed. The blown reveals that the stem has combusted within its node not externally but internally heated so as the stem can lay in formation. Very much akin to the energy process of a microwave oven that uses microwaves to heat the food internally. Once heated the plant lays in patterns in the field, by a process not known but likely to be by electromagnetic fields surrounding the process guided to form the design of the Crop Circle, a technology not yet been developed.

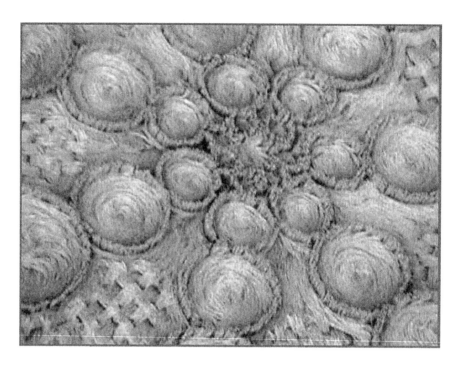

Intricate pattern contained within a Crop Circle.

A magnetic compass placed within a recently formed Crop Circle is shown to act wildly, showing an erratic Electro Magnetic field. The question, what makes Crop Circles? If it is not humanly made then is it naturally formed or is it of an alien intelligence? Who or what makes Crop Circles? The natural answer would be naturally made but because of their intricate intelligent designs, it doubtful. Which seems to lead us to the conclusion extraterrestrial life is the instigator, of these formations. We have film showing the making of one of these Crop Circles and it shows that round orbs of light are responsible. They are possibly an alien drone of some sought.

These balls of light move extremely fast and the Crop Circle above was formed within minutes. We do not know the means of their energy it can only be speculation, but as soon as they have formed the Crop Circle they just as soon disappear only to return to design more. These orbs seem to concentrate their work on ancient sites.

Fig a. Two orbs of light filmed above field.

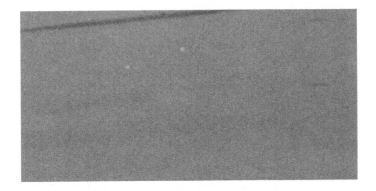

Fig b. Indentations appear in the field.

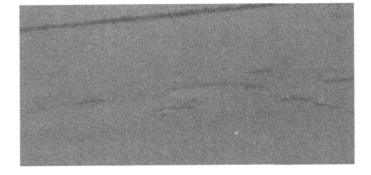

Fig c. The outline of a Crop Circle can be seen forming.

A couple of lights

Stonehenge has seen many Crop Circles.

The vast array of shapes, geometrical patterns and the enormity of the size of these Crop Circles seem to boggle the mind they seem at first to only have the language of metaphor which anybody with an imaginative mind could interpret with many tongues as many ideas, which those listening take as a pinch of salt. I quite frankly steered away from publishing this kind of book, I felt others had covered the phenomena quite adequately but I was left with the feeling that Crop Circles were and are still a mystery. I wanted to know more what these great metaphors of what appeared to be of extraterrestrial origin had to really say. Those that claimed to be able to read them seemed to me the types that could explain the same kind of esoteric art emanating from the modern art museums.

In researching this Crop Circle activity I have noticed a change in their frequency in 2017. The formations had their climax in the last decade and looking over the Crop Circle formations in 2017, gone are the vast, jaw dropping, complicated geometrical patterns of former years that just dazzled the mind. But instead were replaced with a mediocre display, the simpler patterns of the early eighties. A reappraisal moment perhaps I see there is a noticeable return to a simpler mode of expression perhaps we of this generation might interpret. This was the catalyst for this work to try to understand these simpler shapes to shed light on these simpler formations. The number of them has depleted rapidly since 2016, but this depletion enabled me to take a closer look at the whole and find that through design contained fundamental information pertaining to our earth. I needed a means to interpret this I believe extraterrestrial message I found it in the pseudo science that traced its roots all the way back to Babylon, Egypt, Greece and Rome. The science of astrology the language of the stars mans first attempt to understand the universe.

With each, new crop materialization I drew up an astrological chart showing the positions of the planets, the Sun and Moon on the day that the formation in the fields was discovered. The areas these circles mostly appeared were found to be in the Netherlands and in Wiltshire, Warwickshire, Essex and other sites in England. It has to be noted that over 90% of these crop formations occur in these locations. We do not know why this is the case but these places have historical roots of ancients mounds and temples that are the oldest in the world. Also because of the proliferation of wheat, barley, oilseed rape and grass grown in these areas, it might be the type of canvas the creators of these Crop Circles need, for their technology to reproduce them. For instance, if they were done in the sand surrounding the pyramid in Egypt for instance they would not remain long before blown away, before people had a chance to examine them indeed that appears to be their objective for creation. For us as a race to recognize what the most advanced civilizations in the universe have to tell us about our own world and our place in it to help us depart from the eve of our own destruction by working along with the natural forces that are contained in the universe that pertain to our very survival on this our planet earth. Those scoffing the stars can have any influence on us will necessary bear in mind it is the most advanced civilizations in the universe that reveal to us this fact, too work with the natural forces around us to enable us to expand our spiritual consciousness to think, what have people to gain if they dead have lost the means of obtaining to their true self.

With detrimental human activity, resulting environmental damage, the loss of natural habitats and species all a ruination to our planet. The hope seems impossible but our children are our hope and it is only through them our planet secured, it after all belongs to them. The hopelessness of the last generation need not be visited on them they have the means to choose to make a choice. Sadly, and all too evidently we like sheep rather not make. But in time circumstances will be forced upon us. They the creators of these circles that you will find in this small book are a reflection of that hope that their message will be understood that we too are all children of the stars.

Author

CHAPTER ONE

CROP CIRCLES IN APRIL 2017

We are going to examine chronologically those Crop Circles that appeared in 2017. Those reported by people to Crop Circle Center which is the largest internet data base site for logging Crop Circles. Their data goes back years. But we shall be concentrating on just the one year, to try and make some sense out of the phenomena. I understand some readers will be new to this but we are dealing with cosmic patterns revealed in our solar system. These patterns are well known to those who have studied the ancient science of astrology. The pseudo-science that states what happens above shall have its consequence below on this our earth. This appears to be what the makers of the Crop Circles are revealing to us that we are interconnected through the planetary dynamics of our solar system.

We begin with the first reported sighting of a Crop Circle in 2017. Often they appear in early March or April and finish in September. The first Crop Circle appears in the Netherlands, a very simple one it just the design of a circle, like the early Crop Circle designs in the 80's. They progressively get more complicated as we progress through the year. We are led very slowly like a child in kinder garden to learn the fundamentals first the A,B,C of this knowledge.

When we look to the sky the first design we see is a circle, the sun or Moon, the stars, the planets through a telescope. Thus the circle tells us we are to look at an orb in the sky, which orb will become clear as we progress with this knowledge. There is going to appear symbols that the reader may find strange but it is the way this hidden knowledge is presented. I will explain latter as we progress.

THE NETHERLANDS 10TH APRIL 2017

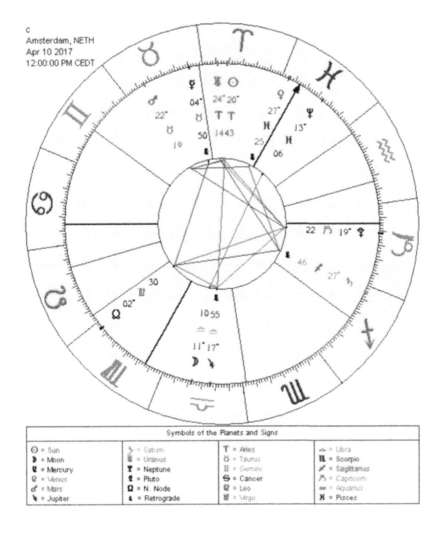

c
Amsterdam, NETH
Apr 10 2017
12:00:00 PM CEDT

Symbols of the Planets and Signs			
☉ = Sun	♄ = Saturn	♈ = Aries	♎ = Libra
☽ = Moon	♅ = Uranus	♉ = Taurus	♏ = Scorpio
☿ = Mercury	♆ = Neptune	♊ = Gemini	♐ = Sagittarius
♀ = Venus	♇ = Pluto	♋ = Cancer	♑ = Capricorn
♂ = Mars	☊ = N. Node	♌ = Leo	♒ = Aquarius
♃ = Jupiter	⚡ = Retrograde	♍ = Virgo	♓ = Pisces

The above chart shows the planetary positions and their angles on the 10th April 2017. We are told to look at the orb that is a circle. That is our star the Sun which is positioned at 20 degrees in Aries. Something will happen to the Sun this year indeed a solar eclipse.

Angles are the dynamics between planets and the Sun and Moon in the sky. These are divided into the semi-sextile 30 degrees, the sextile 60 degrees, the square 90 degrees, the trine 120 degrees and the opposition 180 degrees. The orb angles as seen from the Earth.

THE NETHERLANDS 12TH APRIL 2017

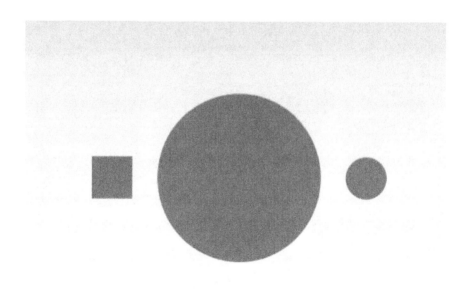

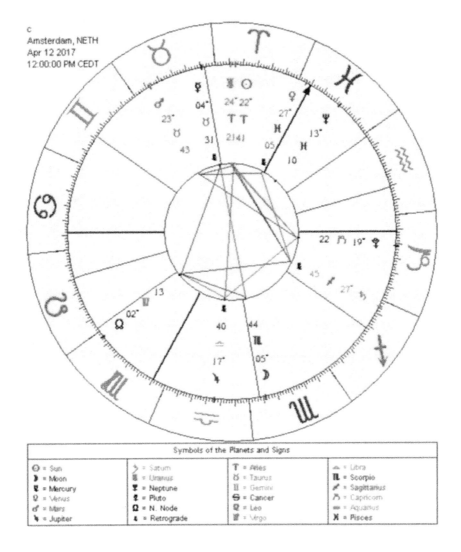

Symbols of the Planets and Signs			
☉ = Sun	♄ = Saturn	♈ = Aries	♎ = Libra
☽ = Moon	♅ = Uranus	♉ = Taurus	♏ = Scorpio
☿ = Mercury	♆ = Neptune	♊ = Gemini	♐ = Sagittarius
♀ = Venus	♇ = Pluto	♋ = Cancer	♑ = Capricorn
♂ = Mars	☊ = N. Node	♌ = Leo	♒ = Aquarius
♃ = Jupiter	⚷ = Retrograde	♍ = Virgo	♓ = Pisces

The larger disc is the sun followed by a much smaller orb. But which orb connects with the sun? We are shown in the shape that is a square, the 90 degree angle between another planetary orb, in our solar system this must be the outer planetary orb Pluto. The Sun at 22 degrees Aries, squares (90 degrees) Pluto at 19 degrees Capricorn this tells us we are having an intelligent communication.

CHERHILL WILTSHIRE 16TH APRIL 2017

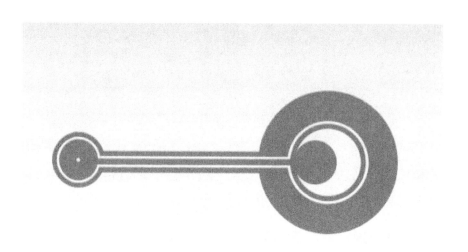

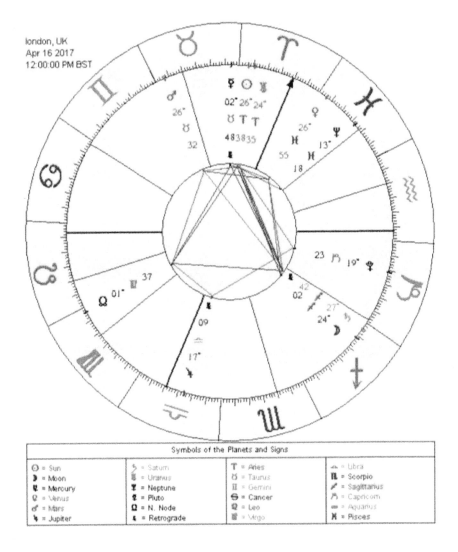

london, UK
Apr 16 2017
12:00:00 PM BST

Symbols of the Planets and Signs			
☉ = Sun	♄ = Saturn	♈ = Aries	♎ = Libra
☽ = Moon	♅ = Uranus	♉ = Taurus	♏ = Scorpio
☿ = Mercury	♆ = Neptune	♊ = Gemini	♐ = Sagittarius
♀ = Venus	♇ = Pluto	♋ = Cancer	♑ = Capricorn
♂ = Mars	☊ = N. Node	♌ = Leo	♒ = Aquarius
♃ = Jupiter	℞ = Retrograde	♍ = Virgo	♓ = Pisces

In this Crop Circle formation we have eclipsed planetary bodies and when we look at our chart above we the Moon is at 24 degrees Sagittarius and eclipsing Saturn 27 degrees Sagittarius. In the Crop Circle we see it pointing to a horse a hill figure on Cherhill Down, 3.5 miles east of Calne in Wiltshire, England. The direction of the Crop Circle helps us in the understanding of its communication. Sagittarius, half human and half horse, is the centaur of mythology.

This transit of the moon and Saturn is in Sagittarius (♐). The conduit with the orb with a dot could be the approaching transit.

TARLTON DOWN GLOUCESTERSHIRE 18TH APRIL 2017

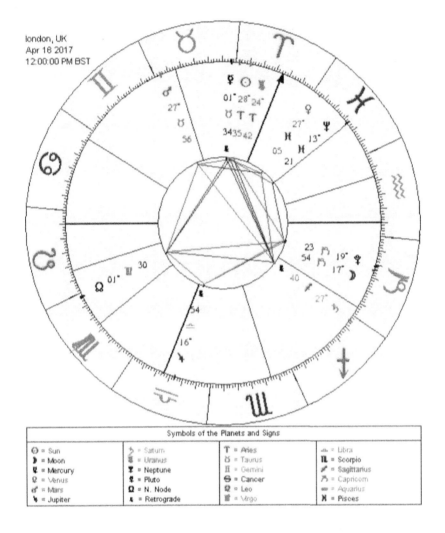

london, UK
Apr 18 2017
12:00:00 PM BST

Symbols of the Planets and Signs

☉ = Sun	♄ = Saturn	♈ = Aries	♎ = Libra
☽ = Moon	♅ = Uranus	♉ = Taurus	♏ = Scorpio
☿ = Mercury	♆ = Neptune	♊ = Gemini	♐ = Sagittarius
♀ = Venus	♇ = Pluto	♋ = Cancer	♑ = Capricorn
♂ = Mars	☊ = N. Node	♌ = Leo	♒ = Aquarius
♃ = Jupiter	℞ = Retrograde	♍ = Virgo	♓ = Pisces

In the Crop Circle we see the Moon eclipses a planet. The Moon at 17 degrees Capricorn makes a planetary transit over Pluto at 19 degrees Capricorn. Two smaller bodies are shown one nearer the transit the other is further away, Venus at 27 degrees and Neptune at 13 degrees Pisces making a 60 degree aspect to the moon transit.

THE NETHERLANDS 18TH APRIL 2017

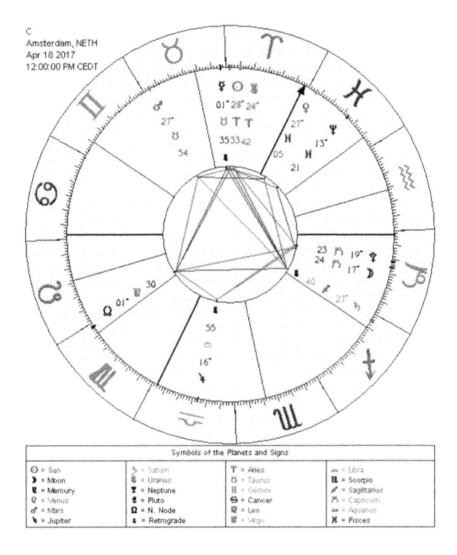

Another view of the Planets for 18th April this time from the Netherlands Crop Circle from right to left, Mercury, Sun, Uranus, Venus, Neptune and Pluto.

OLIVER'S CASTLE WILTSHIRE 24TH APRIL 2017

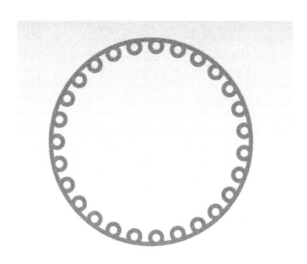

Twenty-seven circles within one large circle

3x3x3=27 9+9+9=27

THE NETHERLANDS 26TH APRIL 2017

A continual of COSMIC KNOWLEDGE from the 18th April Crop Circle in the Netherlands the larger orb must be the sun surrounded by five orbs, the Moon, Mercury, Uranus, Venus and Neptune.

MADRON HOLY WELL CORNWALL 28TH APRIL 2017

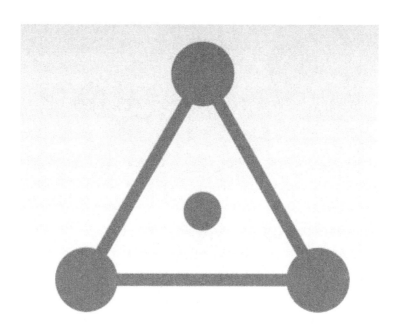

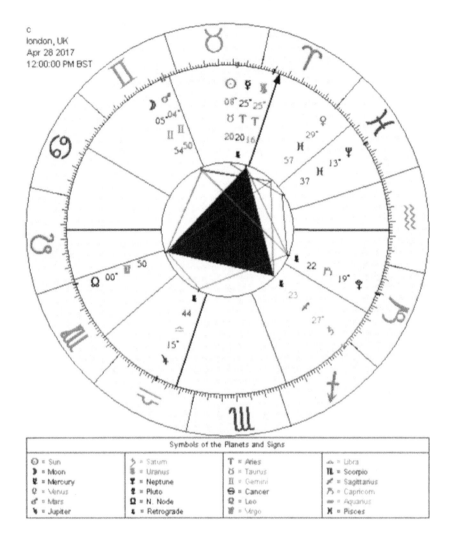

An unmistakable trine of 120 degrees between three points in the Zodiac making a triangle in the circle between Uranus/Mercury at 25 degrees Aries, the North Node at o degrees Virgo and Saturn at 27 degrees Sagittarius. The circle in the middle is our own earth.

CHAPTER TWO

CROP CIRCLES IN MAY 2017

WILLOUGHBY HEDGE WILTSHIRE 4TH MAY 2017

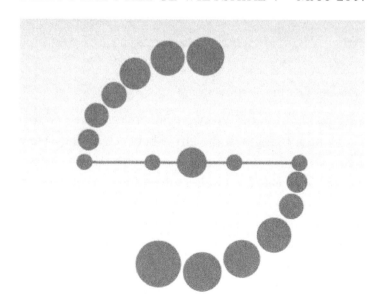

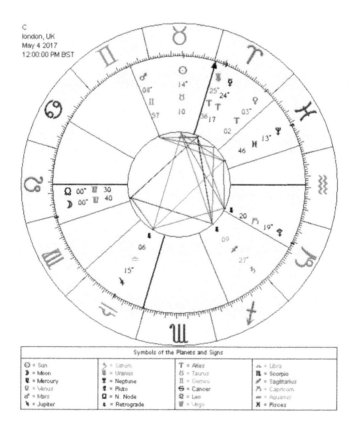

The aliens have given us a cosmic draft of the heavens as of 4th May 2017. Six orbs above the horizon and six orbs below the horizon. In the above chart the horizon stretches from Leo to Aquarius.

Beneath the horizon are~   above the horizon are~

North Node   Neptune

Moon   Venus

Jupiter   Mercury

Saturn   Uranus

Pluto   Sun

(Missing planet?)   Mars

THE NETHERLANDS 11TH MAY 2017

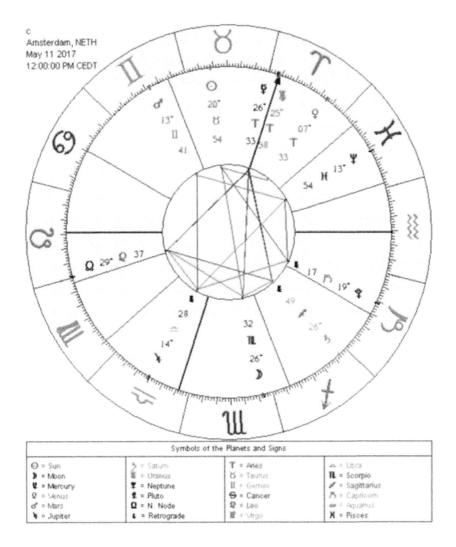

An unmistakable trine of 120 degrees between three points in the Zodiac making a triangle in the circle between Uranus/Mercury at 25/26 degrees Aries, the North Node at 29 degrees Leo and Saturn at 26 degrees Sagittarius. The circle in the middle is our own earth.

This information was also left in the Crop Circle at Madron, Holy Well in Cornwall on 28th April 2017.

THE NETHERLANDS 18TH MAY 2017

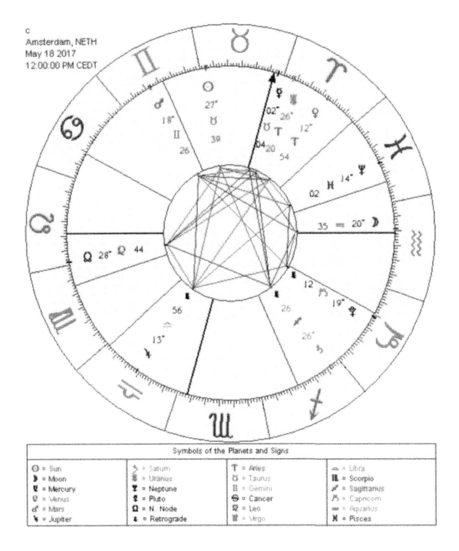

Symbols of the Planets and Signs

☉ = Sun	♄ = Saturn	♈ = Aries	♎ = Libra
☽ = Moon	♅ = Uranus	♉ = Taurus	♏ = Scorpio
☿ = Mercury	♆ = Neptune	♊ = Gemini	♐ = Sagittarius
♀ = Venus	♇ = Pluto	♋ = Cancer	♑ = Capricorn
♂ = Mars	☊ = N. Node	♌ = Leo	♒ = Aquarius
♃ = Jupiter	↟ = Retrograde	♍ = Virgo	♓ = Pisces

The large orb is the sun, the second largest the moon sitting on the horizon along with the spray of eight planets in our solar system.

THE NETHERLANDS 18TH MAY 2017

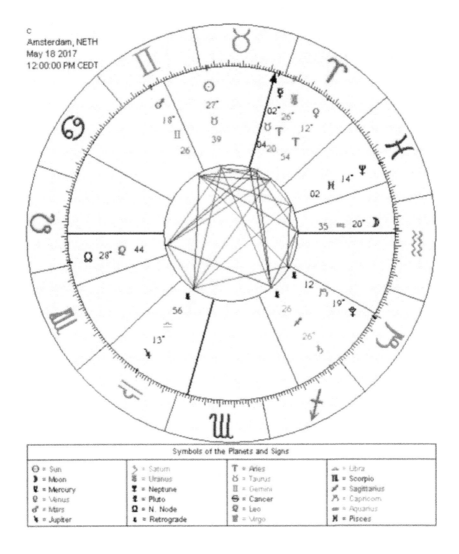

The EXTRATERRESTRIALS tell us to look at the sun, the largest orb surrounded by four planets, Mars, Mercury, Uranus and Venus.

STITCHCOMBE WILTSHIRE 21ST MAY 2017

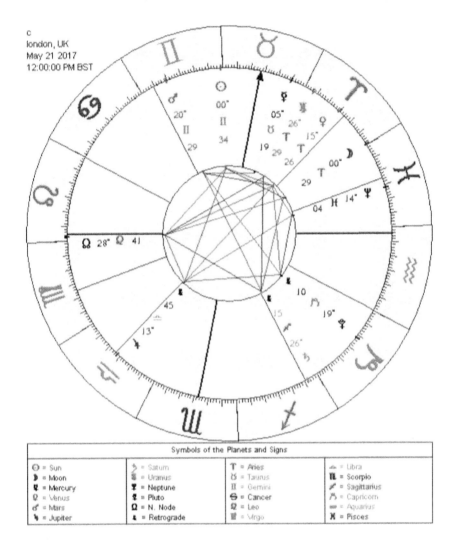

Symbols of the Planets and Signs			
☉ = Sun	♄ = Saturn	♈ = Aries	♎ = Libra
☽ = Moon	♅ = Uranus	♉ = Taurus	♏ = Scorpio
☿ = Mercury	♆ = Neptune	♊ = Gemini	♐ = Sagittarius
♀ = Venus	♇ = Pluto	♋ = Cancer	♑ = Capricorn
♂ = Mars	☊ = N. Node	♌ = Leo	♒ = Aquarius
♃ = Jupiter	☍ = Retrograde	♍ = Virgo	♓ = Pisces

Look at the Moon they say, enclosing and wrapped by two 12 striped circles. The Moon in the chart is at 00 degrees Aries.

Notice that the Moon will soon transit over Venus in Aries.

DORSET 22ND MAY 2017

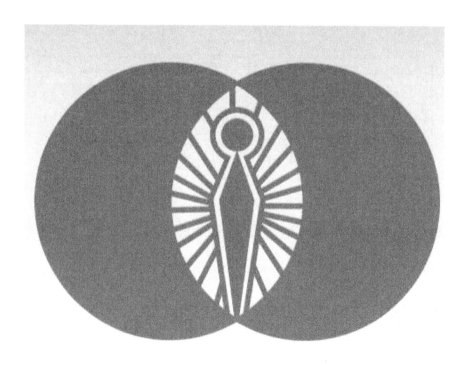

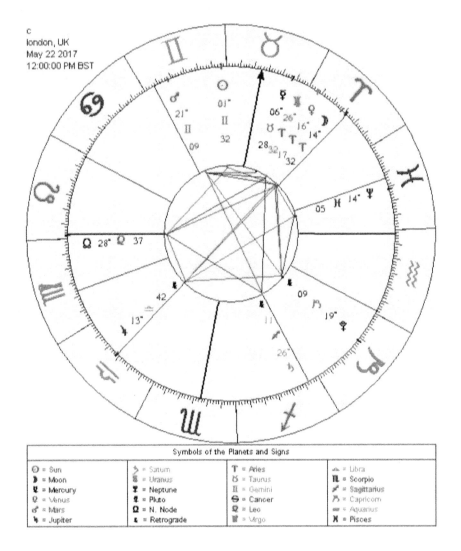

c
london, UK
May 22 2017
12:00:00 PM BST

Symbols of the Planets and Signs

☉ = Sun	♄ = Saturn	♈ = Aries	♎ = Libra
☽ = Moon	♅ = Uranus	♉ = Taurus	♏ = Scorpio
☿ = Mercury	♆ = Neptune	♊ = Gemini	♐ = Sagittarius
♀ = Venus	♇ = Pluto	♋ = Cancer	♑ = Capricorn
♂ = Mars	☊ = N. Node	♌ = Leo	♒ = Aquarius
♃ = Jupiter	↾ = Retrograde	♍ = Virgo	♓ = Pisces

The Moon at 14 degrees Aries transits over Venus at 16 degrees
Aries. The meaning of this Crop Circle is the radiation of Love. By
its shape it is clearly female, symbolic of Venus the planet of Love.

CORNWALL 24ᵀᴴ MAY 2017

Pleiades

The Crop Circle shows what the aliens love, their home. We have a craft travelling to seven stars, four circles showing planets. This looks like the Pleiades, in Taurus the Seven Sisters. It is among the nearest star clusters to Earth and is the cluster most obvious to the naked eye in the night sky.

So far so good, they have described the solar system of how they observe it that corresponds with our own knowledge on earth, we have agreement. I can understand the rudiments. Now things will turn to get a little more complicated and I have to be honest some things I just cannot understand, but I will do my best to translate.

WILTSHIRE 25TH MAY 2017

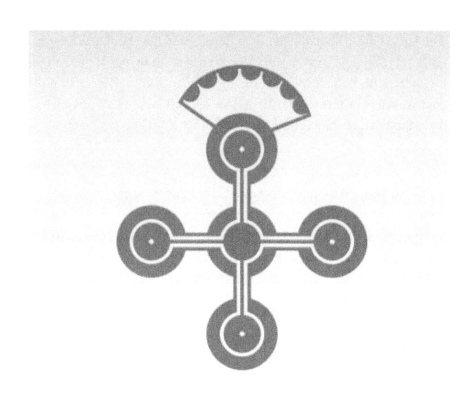

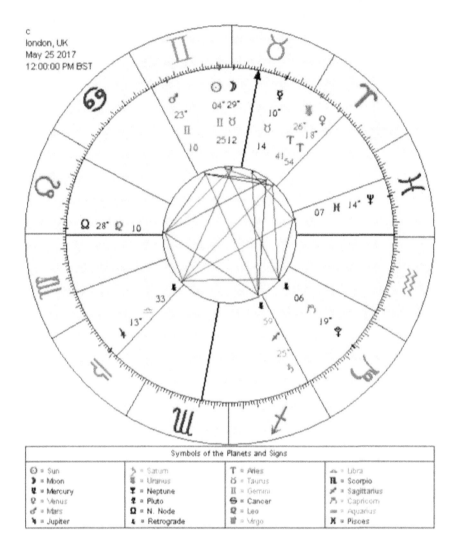

c
london, UK
May 25 2017
12:00:00 PM BST

Symbols of the Planets and Signs			
☉ = Sun	♄ = Saturn	♈ = Aries	♎ = Libra
☽ = Moon	♅ = Uranus	♉ = Taurus	♏ = Scorpio
☿ = Mercury	♆ = Neptune	♊ = Gemini	♐ = Sagittarius
♀ = Venus	♇ = Pluto	♋ = Cancer	♑ = Capricorn
♂ = Mars	☊ = N. Node	♌ = Leo	♒ = Aquarius
♃ = Jupiter	☙ = Retrograde	♍ = Virgo	♓ = Pisces

There are four primary cosmic forces acting on the earth, the orb seen in the middle of the formation. The forces arise from the North, South, East and West. Four coordinated points form a cross. It is from the northern force we have seven planets connected to it.

These seven planets left to right are Mars, Sun, Moon, Mercury, Uranus, Venus and Neptune.

HAMPSHIRE 25TH MAY 2017

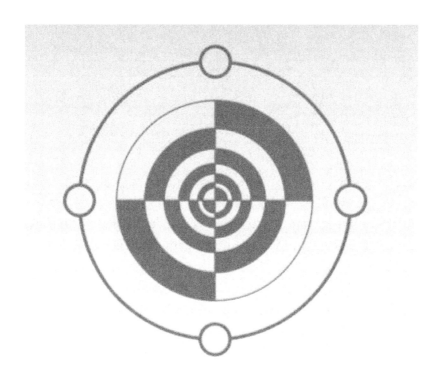

The extraterrestrials have concentrated us on the four points in ancient astrology known as Ascendant, Descendant, MC, and IC.

BASICS OF ASTROLOGICAL FORCES

Your **Rising** Sign, otherwise known as an **Ascendant**, is the **Zodiac** Sign that was**rising** on the eastern horizon at the moment you were born. It can be abbreviated on a birth chart as ASC or AS. ... The **Ascendant** is said to be the mask one wears in public... it is the first impression we make when we meet new people.

The **descendant** forms the cusp of the seventh house of the horoscope and refers to partners or relationships. The **descendant** is ruled by the seventh **sign** of the zodiac, Libra, and its ruler planet, Venus.

The **Midheaven** (MC or Medium Coeli, literally 'middle of the sky') is one of the most important angles in the birth chart. It traditionally indicates career, status, aim in life, aspirations, public reputation, and our life goal.

In astrology, the **Imum Coeli** (Latin for "bottom of the sky"), IC, is the point in space where the ecliptic crosses the meridian in the north, exactly opposite the Midheaven. It marks the fourth house cusp in most house systems (this is reversed in the southern hemisphere).

WILTSHIRE 28TH MAY 2017

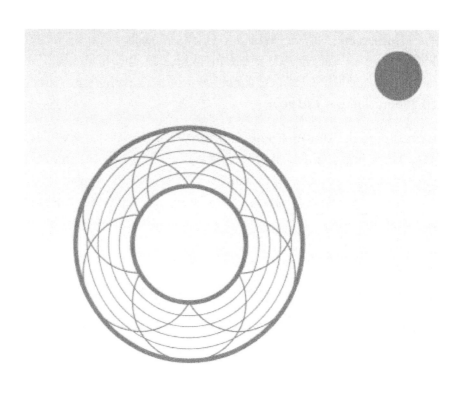

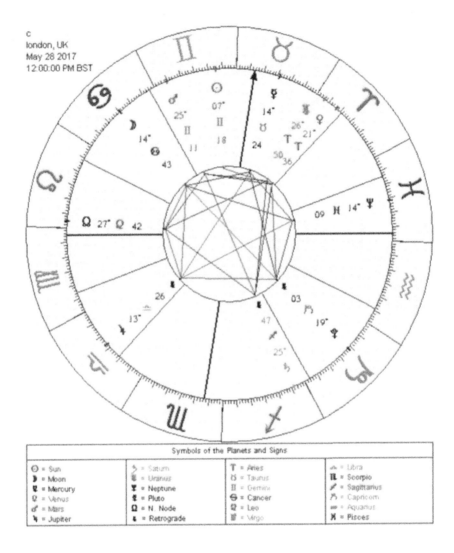

A circle with five inner circles, the number five (5) in astrology equates to the planet Mercury and this planet is shown as an orb outside the large circle. The aliens are telling us to concentrate on Mercury it is positioned at 14 degrees Taurus in the chart above. I have a feeling they are going to reveal something very wonderful.

WILTSHIRE 28TH MAY 2017

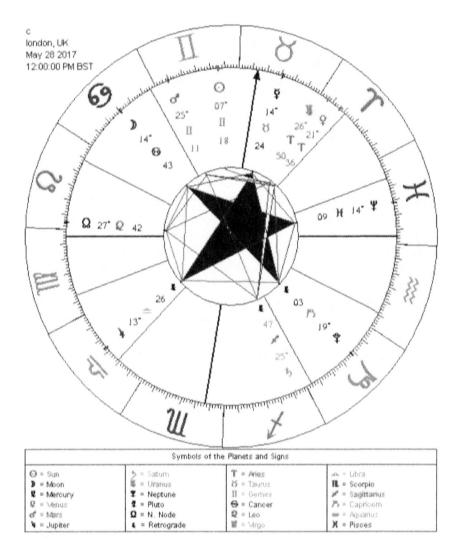

c
london, UK
May 28 2017
12:00:00 PM BST

Symbols of the Planets and Signs			
☉ = Sun	♄ = Saturn	♈ = Aries	♎ = Libra
☽ = Moon	♅ = Uranus	♉ = Taurus	♏ = Scorpio
☿ = Mercury	♆ = Neptune	♊ = Gemini	♐ = Sagittarius
♀ = Venus	♇ = Pluto	♋ = Cancer	♑ = Capricorn
♂ = Mars	☊ = N. Node	♌ = Leo	♒ = Aquarius
♃ = Jupiter	⚡ = Retrograde	♍ = Virgo	♓ = Pisces

A five pointed star. Starting from Mercury at 14 degrees Taurus, the other points are Moon at 14 degrees Cancer, Jupiter at 13 degrees Libra, Pluto at 19 degrees Capricorn and finally, Neptune at 14 degrees Pisces forming the five-stared Pentacle in the sky. I am astonished also there are nine orbs each surrounded by four smaller orbs and five orbs surrounded by twenty smaller orbs. In the seals of Solomon the first pentacle of Mercury is represented by a pentacle it conveys personal magnetism to the owner. It serves to invoke the spirits who are under the firmament, me and you, us.

WILTSHIRE 30TH MAY 2017

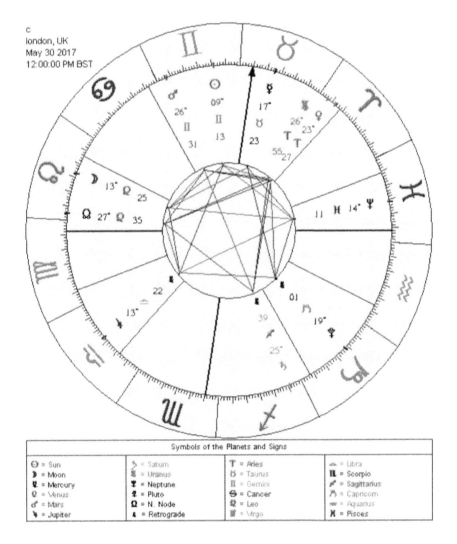

A flower that forms a hexagram with six points, the number six is symbolic of Venus. Yet there is a central orb that makes the total of seven orbs, the number seven is symbolic of the orb Neptune. In astrology it is a spiritual planet, now take note of it for a teaching.

Neptune in the chart is positioned at 14 degrees Pisces.

CHAPTER THREE

CROP CIRCLES IN JUNE 2017

WILTSHIRE 3RD JUNE 2017

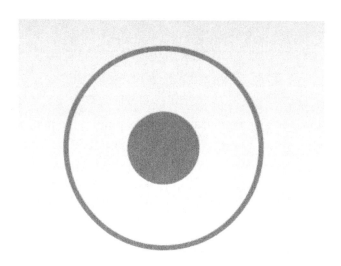

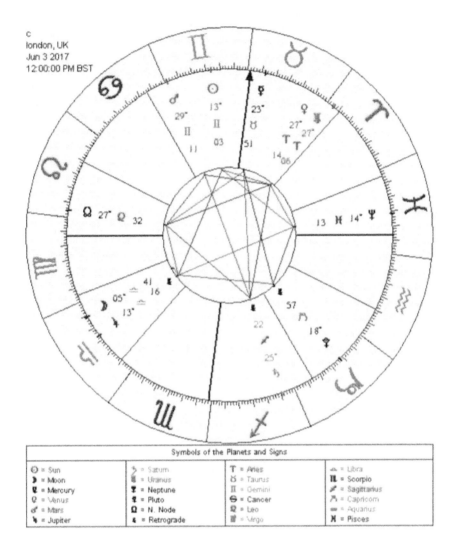

c
london, UK
Jun 3 2017
12:00:00 PM BST

Symbols of the Planets and Signs			
☉ = Sun	♄ = Saturn	♈ = Aries	♎ = Libra
☽ = Moon	♅ = Uranus	♉ = Taurus	♏ = Scorpio
☿ = Mercury	♆ = Neptune	♊ = Gemini	♐ = Sagittarius
♀ = Venus	♇ = Pluto	♋ = Cancer	♑ = Capricorn
♂ = Mars	☊ = N. Node	♌ = Leo	♒ = Aquarius
♃ = Jupiter	☟ = Retrograde	♍ = Virgo	♓ = Pisces

The dot in a circle is complete spiritual oneness a consciousness of the whole that can be achieved through the influence of Neptune. The breaking down of material barriers, that leaves one in space filled with an ecstasy seen in the conjunction of Venus and Uranus at 27 degrees Aries governed by Mars the energy to bring it about.

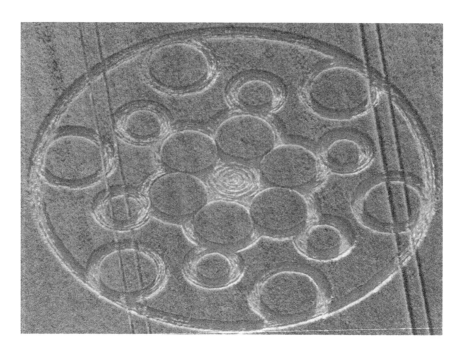

OXFORDSHIRE 4TH JUNE 2017

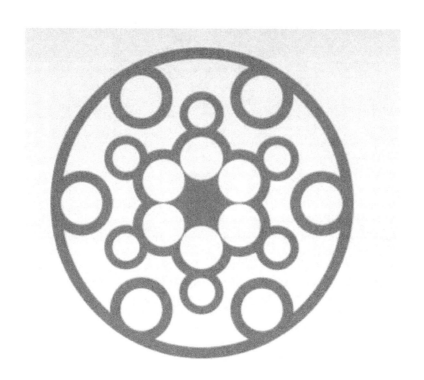

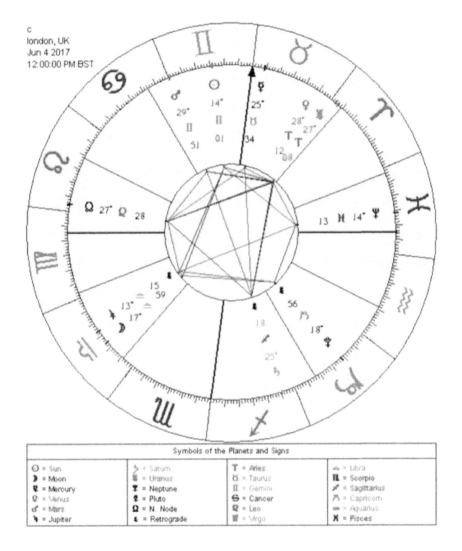

c
london, UK
Jun 4 2017
12:00:00 PM BST

Symbols of the Planets and Signs			
☉ = Sun	♄ = Saturn	♈ = Aries	♎ = Libra
☽ = Moon	♅ = Uranus	♉ = Taurus	♏ = Scorpio
☿ = Mercury	♆ = Neptune	♊ = Gemini	♐ = Sagittarius
♀ = Venus	♇ = Pluto	♋ = Cancer	♑ = Capricorn
♂ = Mars	☊ = N. Node	♌ = Leo	♒ = Aquarius
♃ = Jupiter	℞ = Retrograde	♍ = Virgo	♓ = Pisces

Eighteen circles in one large circle.

6+6+6 = 18

We are now told by the aliens to look now at the planet showing 18 degrees in the heavens. That is Pluto at 18 degrees Capricorn for an important spiritual lesson based on the influence of the cosmos.

WILTSHIRE 9TH JUNE 2017

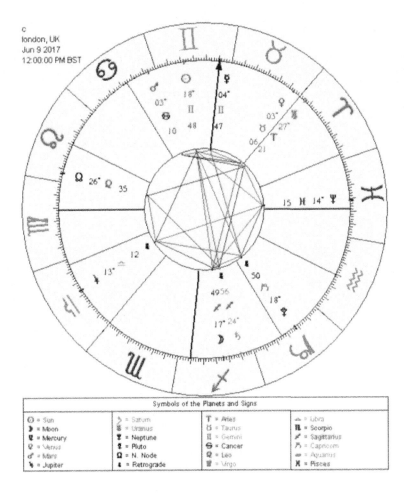

Symbols of the Planets and Signs			
☉ = Sun	♄ = Saturn	♈ = Aries	♎ = Libra
☽ = Moon	♅ = Uranus	♉ = Taurus	♏ = Scorpio
☿ = Mercury	♆ = Neptune	♊ = Gemini	♐ = Sagittarius
♀ = Venus	♇ = Pluto	♋ = Cancer	♑ = Capricorn
♂ = Mars	☊ = N. Node	♌ = Leo	♒ = Aquarius
♃ = Jupiter	℞ = Retrograde	♍ = Virgo	♓ = Pisces

Pluto at 18 degrees Capricorn makes an exact 150 degree aspect to
the sun at 18 degrees Gemini. This aspect is known as a quincunx.
The in-conjunct or quincunx (the terms are generally used
interchangeably) aspect in astrology is formed between orbs that
are roughly 150 degrees apart. The orbs and points involved in a
quincunx don't understand each other. Unless it's an out-of-sign
quincunx, the signs not only are of a different element, they are
also of a different modality. For example, take Capricorn-Gemini.
Here Capricorn is a fixed earth sign, while Gemini is a Mutable air
sign. It's difficult to see common ground between the two they are
two different ways or conflict of being the problem with our earth.
How are we going to resolve this, the aliens are about to show us.
It is an astonishing solution and its knowledge of Jewish teachings.

DORSET 16TH JUNE 2017

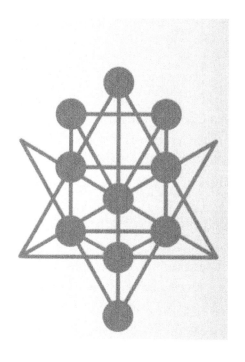

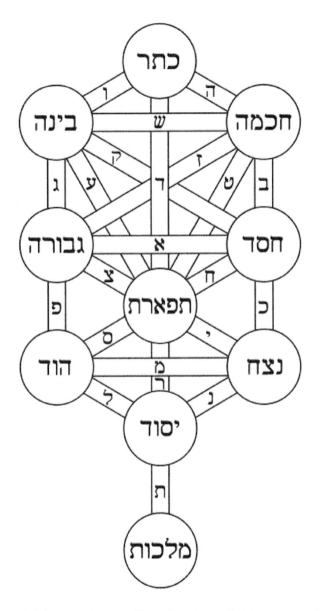

Kabbalah (Hebrew: קַבָּלָה⬜, literally "parallel/corresponding," or "received tradition) is an esoteric method, discipline, and school of thought that originated in Judaism. A traditional Kabbalist in Judaism is called a *Mekubbal*(מְקוּבָּל⬜).

Kabbalah seeks to define the nature of the universe and the human being, the nature and purpose of existence, it also presents methods to aid understanding and thereby attain spiritual realization.

HAMPSHIRE 17TH JUNE 2017

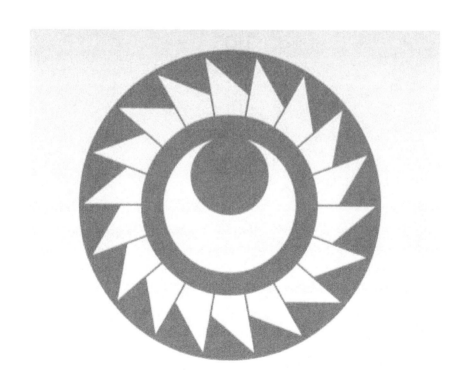

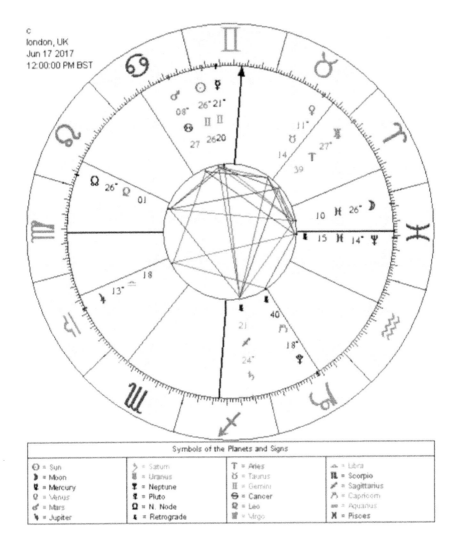

c
london, UK
Jun 17 2017
12:00:00 PM BST

Symbols of the Planets and Signs

☉ = Sun	♄ = Saturn	♈ = Aries	♎ = Libra
☽ = Moon	♅ = Uranus	♉ = Taurus	♏ = Scorpio
☿ = Mercury	♆ = Neptune	♊ = Gemini	♐ = Sagittarius
♀ = Venus	♇ = Pluto	♋ = Cancer	♑ = Capricorn
♂ = Mars	☊ = N. Node	♌ = Leo	♒ = Aquarius
♃ = Jupiter	℞ = Retrograde	♍ = Virgo	♓ = Pisces

A planetary transit with 18 rays sprouting forth. The 18th degree is
occupied by Pluto at 18 degrees Capricorn. The Crop Circle looks
like a sun aspect with Pluto, a transit aiding spiritual regeneration.

THE NETHERLANDS 19TH JUNE 2017

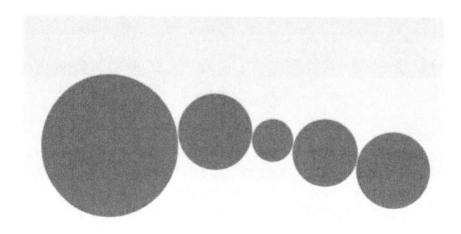

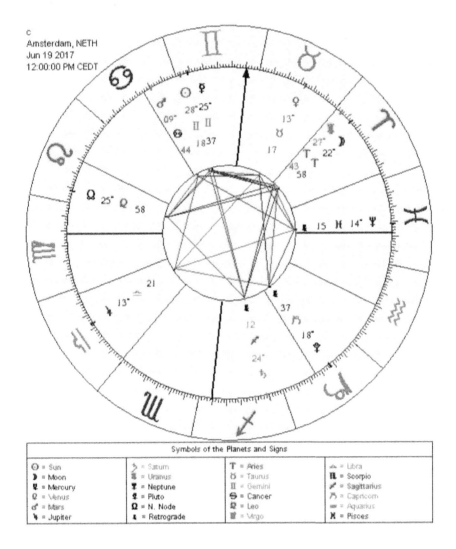

Symbols of the Planets and Signs			
☉ = Sun	♄ = Saturn	♈ = Aries	♎ = Libra
☽ = Moon	♅ = Uranus	♉ = Taurus	♏ = Scorpio
☿ = Mercury	♆ = Neptune	♊ = Gemini	♐ = Sagittarius
♀ = Venus	♇ = Pluto	♋ = Cancer	♑ = Capricorn
♂ = Mars	☊ = N. Node	♌ = Leo	♒ = Aquarius
♃ = Jupiter	℞ = Retrograde	♍ = Virgo	♓ = Pisces

Now look at these five planets! Mars, sun, mercury, venus and Uranus. We are shown by extraterrestrials. Evidently we are going to be given a new teaching.

WILTSHIRE 21ST JUNE 2017

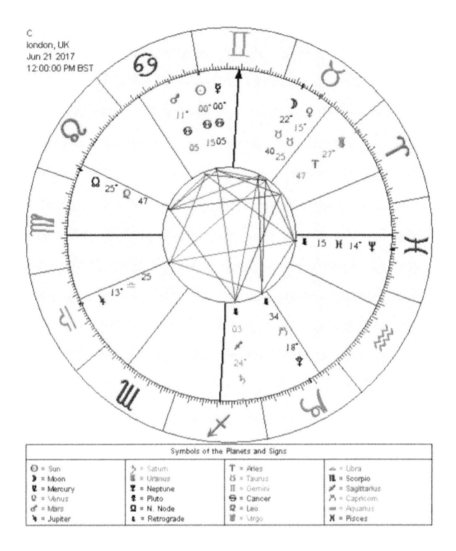

A small circle with a large circle the smaller is joined by a conduit to the large circle perimeter. Two orbs joined and in the chart we see both the sun and Mercury 00 degrees Cancer in transit. Among the five orbs this transit is what we are to look at for the teaching.

WILTSHIRE 26TH JUNE 2017

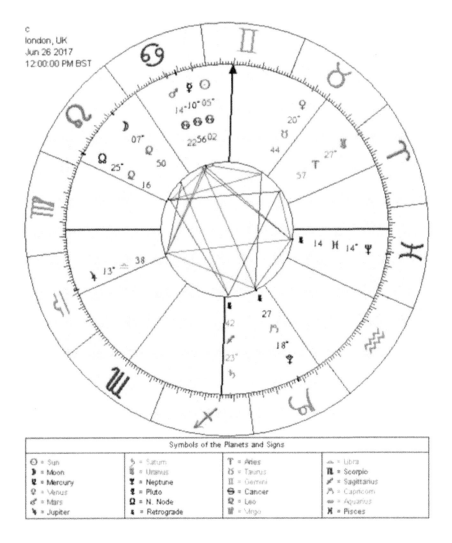

c
london, UK
Jun 26 2017
12:00:00 PM BST

Symbols of the Planets and Signs			
☉ = Sun	♄ = Saturn	♈ = Aries	♎ = Libra
☽ = Moon	♅ = Uranus	♉ = Taurus	♏ = Scorpio
☿ = Mercury	♆ = Neptune	♊ = Gemini	♐ = Sagittarius
♀ = Venus	♇ = Pluto	♋ = Cancer	♑ = Capricorn
♂ = Mars	☊ = N. Node	♌ = Leo	♒ = Aquarius
♃ = Jupiter	ↄ = Retrograde	♍ = Virgo	♓ = Pisces

The smaller orb in the middle of the configuration being shown to us is Mercury joined by the force of the sun to the right and that of Mars to the left. These are cosmic forces acting together to form a powerful dynamic in the heaven that will have impact on the earth.

CHAPTER FOUR

CROP CIRCLES IN JULY 2017

WILTSHIRE 1ST JULY 2017

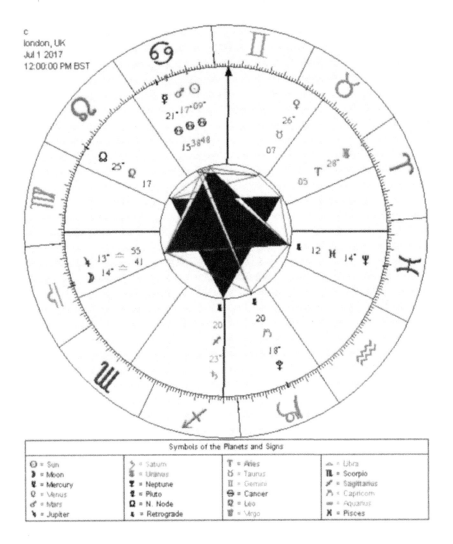

The cube is symbolic of our earth surrounded by the cosmic forces above especially from the conjunction of Mars, Mercury and sun activating all the other planets in the solar system.

WILTSHIRE 1ST JULY 2017

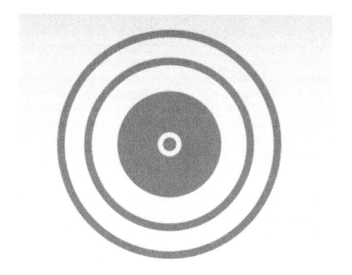

A small circle within a circle is Mercury orbiting the sun, the outer two rings being the orbits of Venus and the Earth around the sun.

THE NETHERLANDS 3RD JULY 2017

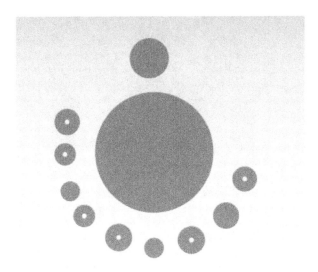

A representation of the solar system ten bodies around the sun the second largest circle being Jupiter.

WILTSHIRE 5TH JULY 2017

This symbol represents four main elements, earth, air, fire, water circled by spirit.

WILTSHIRE 8TH JULY 2017

Twelve quarter circles representing the twelve signs of the zodiac enclosing two inverted triangles symbolizes, as above, so below.

HAMPSHIRE 18TH JULY 2017

Twelve shaded circles representing the twelve signs of the zodiac enclosing two inverted triangles and a cube representing the earth this once again diagrammatically symbolizes, as above, so below.

WEST SUSSEX 19TH JULY 2017

CELTIC CROSS

BEDFORDSHIRE 21ST JULY 2017

PHOENICIAN ALPHABET Q

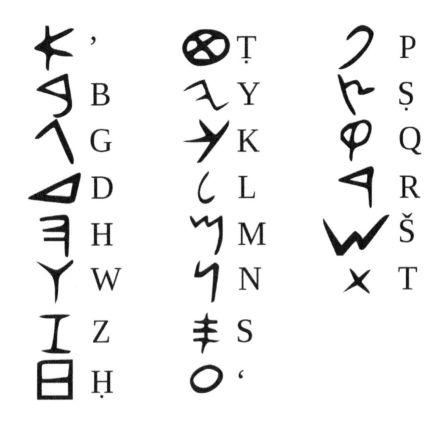

PHOENICIAN ALPHABET

CHAPTER FIVE

CROP CIRCLES IN AUGUST 2017

WILTSHIRE 4TH AUGUST 2017

Half circle circling twelve buds, possibly moon cycle.

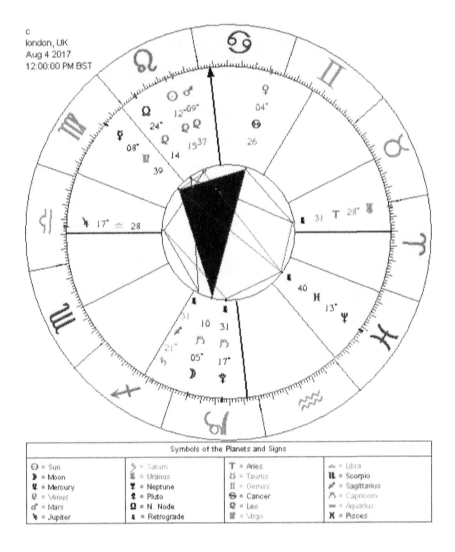

Symbols of the Planets and Signs

☉ = Sun	♄ = Saturn	♈ = Aries	♎ = Libra
☽ = Moon	♅ = Uranus	♉ = Taurus	♏ = Scorpio
☿ = Mercury	♆ = Neptune	♊ = Gemini	♐ = Sagittarius
♀ = Venus	♇ = Pluto	♋ = Cancer	♑ = Capricorn
♂ = Mars	☊ = N. Node	♌ = Leo	♒ = Aquarius
♃ = Jupiter	℞ = Retrograde	♍ = Virgo	♓ = Pisces

The aliens are telling us to look up at the Moon and its phases. It makes an opposition aspect to Venus and a trine aspect to Mercury.

OXFORDSHIRE 5TH AUGUST 2017

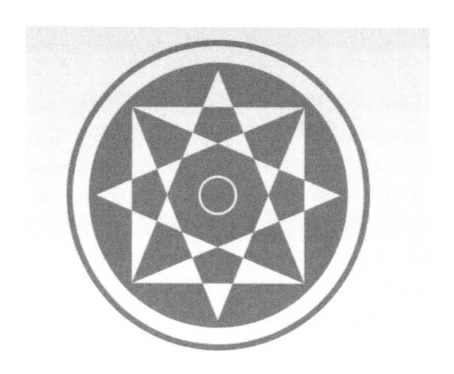

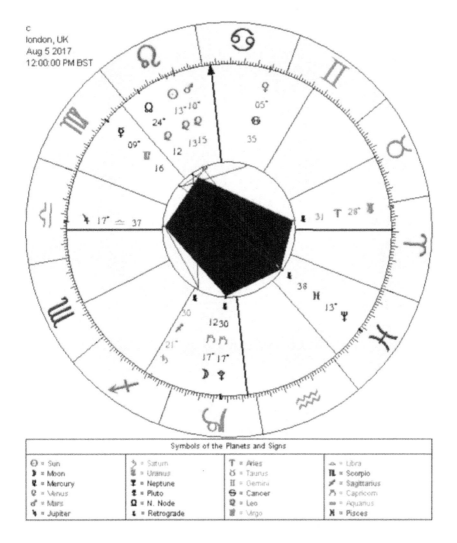

Symbols of the Planets and Signs

☉ = Sun	♄ = Saturn	♈ = Aries	♎ = Libra
☽ = Moon	♅ = Uranus	♉ = Taurus	♏ = Scorpio
☿ = Mercury	♆ = Neptune	♊ = Gemini	♐ = Sagittarius
♀ = Venus	♇ = Pluto	♋ = Cancer	♑ = Capricorn
♂ = Mars	☊ = N. Node	♌ = Leo	♒ = Aquarius
♃ = Jupiter	℞ = Retrograde	♍ = Virgo	♓ = Pisces

Pentagrams that represent the sky above and the degree aspects found between the north node, Jupiter, Pluto, Neptune and Uranus. The message is constant they keep telling us there is a connection through the planets and their aspects to each other to us on earth.

WARWICKSHIRE 7TH AUGUST 2017

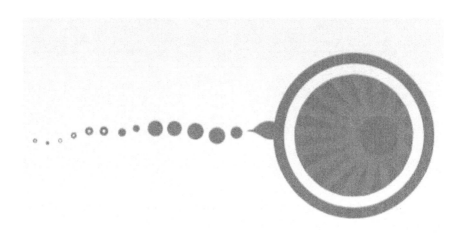

THE SUNLIGHT SEEDS THE TREE FOR GROWTH

ESSEX 17TH AUGUST 2017

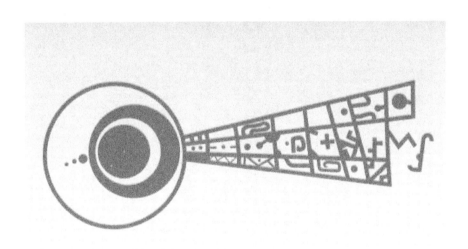

THIS CROP CIRCLE WAS FACING A SIGNAL TOWER

AN ALIEN INSCRIPTION AN ALIEN MESSAGE

Y..S

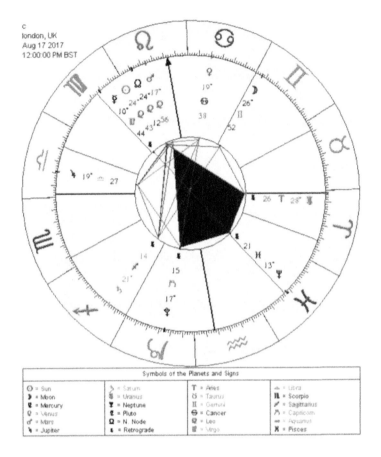

Symbols of the Planets and Signs

☉ = Sun	♄ = Saturn	♈ = Aries	♎ = Libra
☽ = Moon	♅ = Uranus	♉ = Taurus	♏ = Scorpio
☿ = Mercury	♆ = Neptune	♊ = Gemini	♐ = Sagittarius
♀ = Venus	♇ = Pluto	♋ = Cancer	♑ = Capricorn
♂ = Mars	☊ = N. Node	♌ = Leo	♒ = Aquarius
♃ = Jupiter	℞ = Retrograde	♍ = Virgo	♓ = Pisces

Undoubtedly the Crop Circle of 2017 that appeared 17th August, it resembles a key to a door, perhaps the door that opens to the other side of this consciousness. But whatever it is it the resolution to the previous Crop Circle appearing in Warwickshire on the 7th August. In the heavens there is an unmistakable Pyramid symbol. Also we know that pylons hold up the antenna. There are twenty one pylons the first column has 8 pylons the second column 7 pylons the third column 6 pylons and one is blanked, these are the Pylons of Osiris. It is interesting to note the Kabbalah and the twenty-one Pylons of Osiris an ancient Egyptian treatise is connected to the Tree of Life. The message of the children of Pleiades to us is these two systems relate our connectedness to the cosmos its interconnection with us.

THE NETHERLANDS 22ND AUGUST 2017

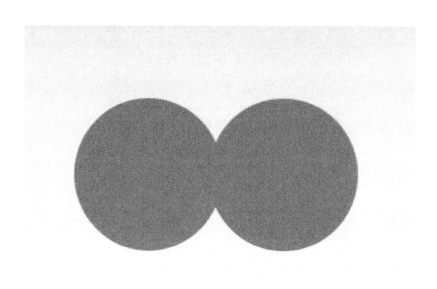

THE SOLAR ECLIPSE OF 22ND AUGUST 2017

THE SOLAR ECLIPSE OF 22ND AUGUST 2017

PEOPLE WEARING PROTECTIVE GLASSES

CHAPTER SIX

CROP CIRCLES IN SEPTEMBER 2017

THE NETHERLANDS 9TH SEPTEMBER 2017

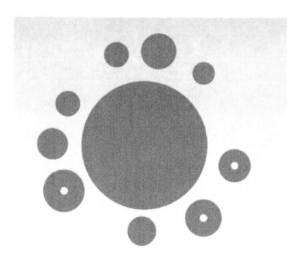

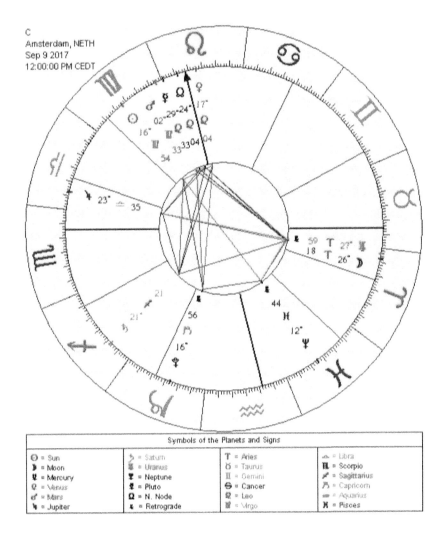

The larger circle the Sun in middle, danced around by three groups of planets.

Mars, Mercury, Venus

Jupiter, Saturn, Pluto

Neptune, Moon, Uranus

THE NETHERLANDS 17TH SEPTEMBER 2017

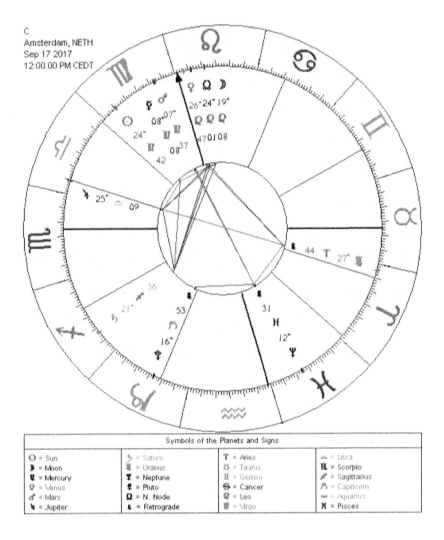

C
Amsterdam, NETH
Sep 17 2017
12:00:00 PM CEDT

Symbols of the Planets and Signs			
☉ = Sun	♄ = Saturn	♈ = Aries	♎ = Libra
☽ = Moon	⛢ = Uranus	♉ = Taurus	♏ = Scorpio
☿ = Mercury	♆ = Neptune	♊ = Gemini	♐ = Sagittarius
♀ = Venus	♇ = Pluto	♋ = Cancer	♑ = Capricorn
♂ = Mars	☊ = N. Node	♌ = Leo	♒ = Aquarius
♃ = Jupiter	℞ = Retrograde	♍ = Virgo	♓ = Pisces

The larger circle the sun leads a group of five orbs or objects

Mercury, Mars, Venus, North Node, Moon.

THE NETHERLANDS 24ᵀᴴ SEPTEMBER 2017

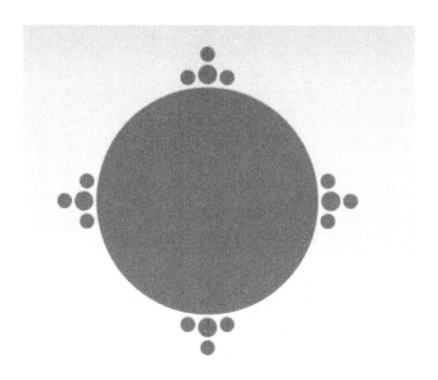

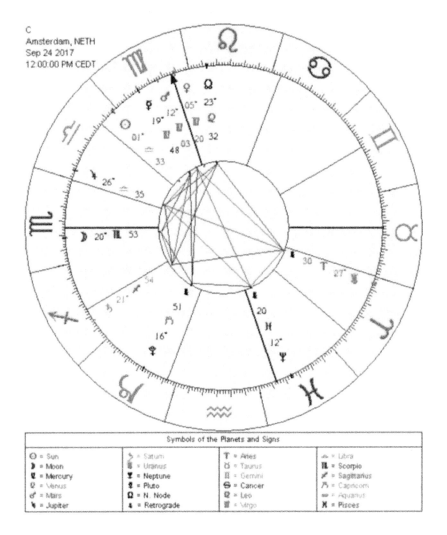

Symbols of the Planets and Signs			
☉ = Sun	♄ = Saturn	♈ = Aries	♎ = Libra
☽ = Moon	♅ = Uranus	♉ = Taurus	♏ = Scorpio
☿ = Mercury	♆ = Neptune	♊ = Gemini	♐ = Sagittarius
♀ = Venus	♇ = Pluto	♋ = Cancer	♑ = Capricorn
♂ = Mars	☊ = N. Node	♌ = Leo	♒ = Aquarius
♃ = Jupiter	⚸ = Retrograde	♍ = Virgo	♓ = Pisces

The larger circle is surrounded by four groups of four representing four movements around the sun therefore we have a depiction of the planet Mercury that revolves around the sun four times a year.

SWITZERLAND 1st OCTOBER 2017

THE YEAR ENDED WITH A FLOWER

It is a law of nature that the microcosm reflects the macrocosm. This is summed up in the Hermetic axiom, 'As above, so below.' Our planetary system consists of one great central fixed star, the Sun, around which the planets revolve in their orbits at varying speeds. From the point of view of an observer standing on one of these planets the Sun will appear to be the moving body and will consequently seem to make a complete circuit of the Zodiac while actually the planet is travelling once around the Sun. This passage, or apparent passage, of the Sun through the twelve signs of the Zodiac is a symbolic equivalent of one whole cycle of experience. Because the aliens are concerned solely with effects on this planet, we on the Earth should base our knowledge on the apparent motion of the Sun and the motion of the planets in relation to our own planet. This is the extraterrestrial knowledge that is imparted to us.

CHAPTER SEVEN

DO WE HAVE CONTACT

The government of course knows of crop circles and are a mystery to them as to us, but they are wary that the messages sent may transform our society from a material based ego centric selfish world to a new world of equality, sharing and harmoniousness. Have we evidence of true communication, yes. In 1974 a digitally encoded message was beamed from a Puerto Rico radio telescope out into space by a team of U.S. SETI astronomers. It was sent as a digitized code that can be reconstructed into an image directed to any life forms that could receive this message. This image included information about our Earth civilization with data about our human body chemistry, our DNA, our height and appearance, our population numbers, our solar system with our sun, and our means of transmitting messages into space.

Chilbolton Glyph, UK   Arecibo, PR, radio image

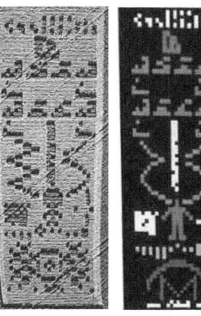

August 20, 2001   November 16, 1974

In August of 2001, an answer was returned to us as a Crop Circle for the world to see. It contained similar information to the one we sent out, from a civilization attempting to communicate with us. To do this, they were somehow able to send their message through a means more advanced than any technology we now possess. In their transmission it appears they say they use telepathy to transmit to us.

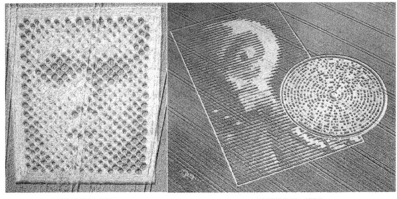

AUGUST 14, 2001   AUGUST 14, 2002

This crop circle of an ET face is formed next to a microwave station. This is giving us a clue about how to contact them with our technology. According to Palden Jenkins, microwave systems are ideal because they offer superior high-speed wideband links for video and digital telecommunication signals to and from space. This medium provides services such as cellular phones, television programming and emergency services.

The 2002 crop circle of the ET face contains a disc that appears to be the same format as a DVD or a CD-ROM disc when looked at under high magnification. Looking at it, you would see blocks representing digital bits of information. The blocks of information are organized as a spiral. These can be decoded into letters and then words.

Beware the bearers of FALSE gifts & their BROKEN PROMISES.

Much PAIN but still time.

There is GOOD out there.

We Oppose DECEPTION.

Conduit CLOSING (BELL SOUND)

CHAPTER EIGHT

THE CROP CIRCLE GALLERY

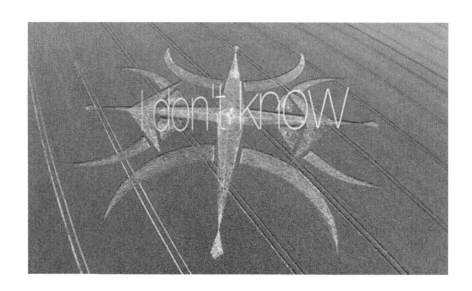

Spotty Flower

Jigsaw Puzzle

Smiley Face

Diamond

A sun with a shell in the middle

Googley eyes

That's actually a snake in a pond

A tiger

Air balloon!

A shepherd

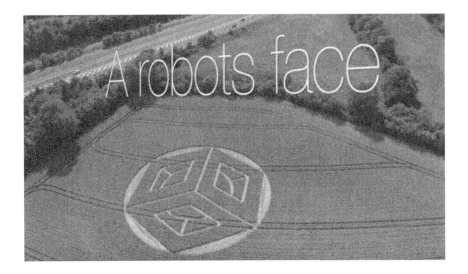

A robots face

Somthing that we put on presents. (a bow)

A hosepipe

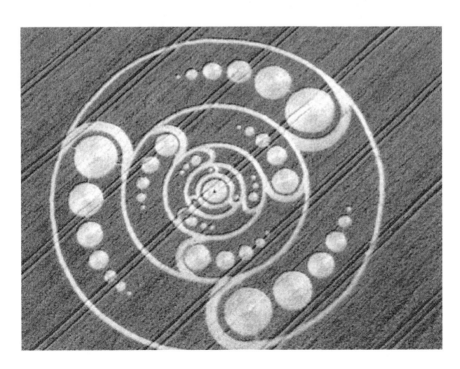

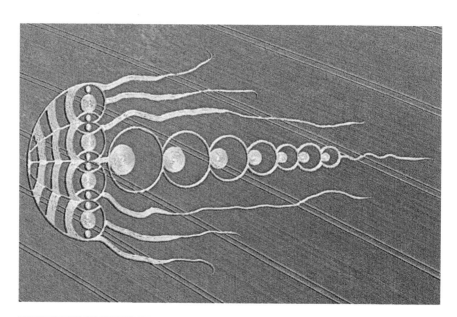

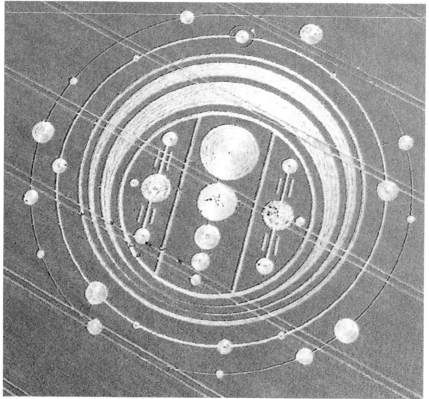

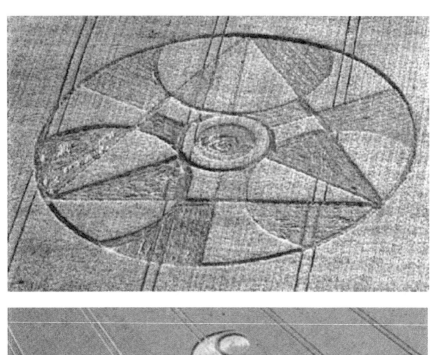

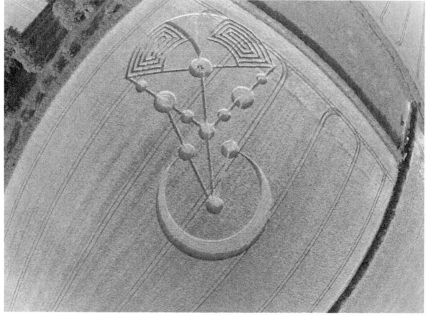

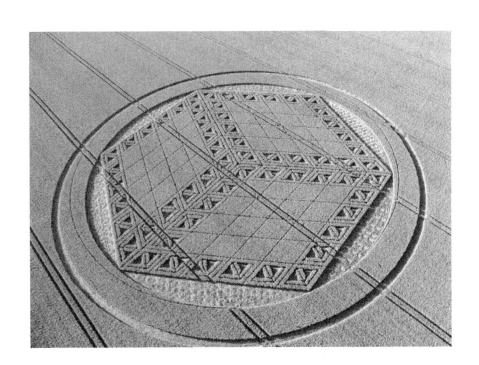

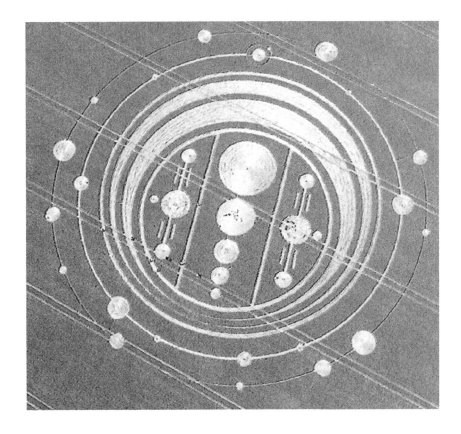

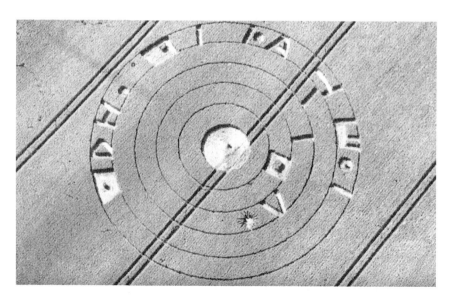

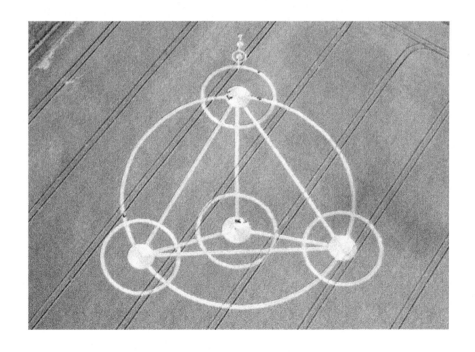

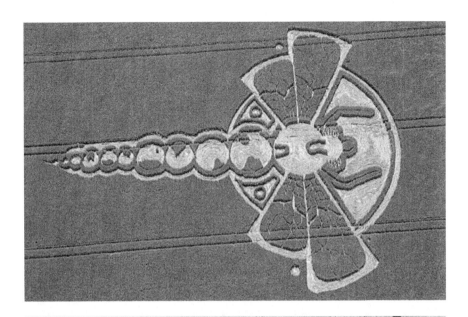

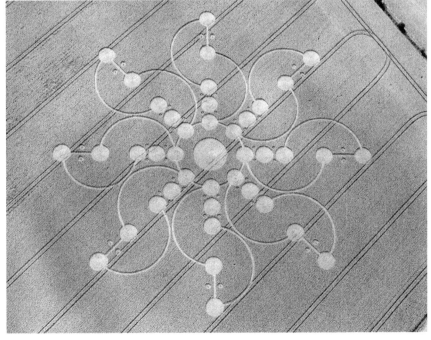

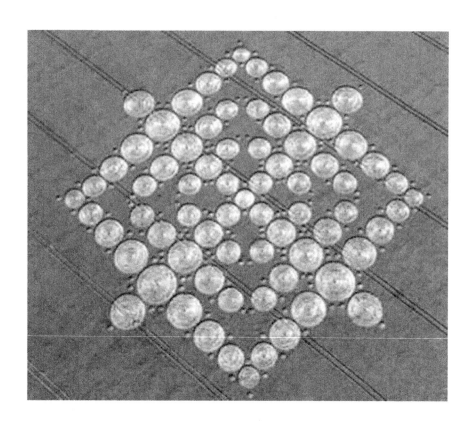

APPENDIX

PEOPLES REACTION TO CROP CIRCLES

I'm the journalist who last week exclusively reported Laurance Rockefeller's decision to fund a study of crop circles. My article for the Western Daily Press of Bristol was seized upon by news agencies around the world and I was amazed to see that this patently man-made creation still exerts such a fascinating hold on the gullible. I've studied crop circles for a decade now in the course of my work as a journalist. I like a good mystery as much as the next man, but these circles are, I have to say, overwhelmingly of human origin. The remainder are the result of freak weather conditions known as mini-vortexes. Sorry Mr Rockefeller: give your money to charity instead.
David Humphrey, UK

Some of the formations are too perfect to be the work of pranksters. I do, however, think that they are the result of natural processes such as magnetic fields, underground archaeology or geology and the wind rather than aliens.
Barry Tregear, England

If aliens have the intelligence to get in and out of earth that many times without being seen, they could certainly come up with something better than a crop circle!
B. Kuzava, USA

Our planet is a marvellous wonder and has secrets that it will never reveal! Freak of nature or out of this world - who knows or ever will know!!
Cathie, England

Piffle. That these things could be anything but people playing the ignorant, superstitious and stupid for fools, is patently silly. If they were really the work of aliens, then what do they represent? A landing zone? How far up can one get above them before they can no longer be seen? Certainly not to the limits of the atmosphere. Are they simply an alien version of 'Kilroy was here?' The fact that

people waste more than a few seconds pondering this issue reinforces my faith in the basic stupidity of mankind.
Jim Hubbell, USA

I tend to have an open mind on most things and if you are inclined to think we are the only ones inhabiting this galaxy you are very naive. Of the 100 billion plus stars this side of the galactic centre, why should ours be the only one to have a rock with life attached floating around it. Also, alien intelligence is likely to be considerably more advanced than ours. Humans have been around for about 15 million years, a blink of an eye in the 5 billion years the Earth has.
I reckon any advanced alien race could warrant no real reason to spend their valuable time seriously interacting with us, like we don't really bother interacting much with say, ants or beetles. But there are some people that catalogue and monitor the progress of ants and beetles etc (why i don't know) so why not catalogue the Earth?
Mark, England

The formation of crop circles goes against all the rules of human logic. However, all you hoax theorists ask yourself this..... what are the rules of an aliens logic?
Paul Marshall, USA

If Crop Circles are made by aliens, it is unlikely that 90% of these are found in Britain. Unless somehow the aliens are extremely fond of Britain. I think Crop Circles are a chapter of "Dr. Who".
Thiam Huat, Singapore

A bunch of hippies with nothing else to do at night except ruin a proportion of farmers' crops, because they have no mates to meet at the pub.
Jonathan Harker, New Zealand

I don't think that the crop circles are a hoax. Some of them look a bit to complex to be manmade. Suppose that the crop circles were made by aliens, wouldn't that be great? A sign from outer space!
Gilbert Koningstein, The Netherlands

Crop circles could well be hoaxes, but shouldn't we investigate why people would want to create them in the first place? Could they be linked to Stonehenge, and what makes people sure that they are related to UFOs? Perhaps they (crop circles) are unmodified gateways between the reality of this universe and a parallel spiritual plain.
Mark Hampson, England

Always the rural folks cooking up such stories. Crop circles are the creation of bored farmers or bored citizens of small towns who are having a laugh at the expense of those fools called UFO enthusiasts. A counter question, if you wanted to communicate with someone far away, would you travel all that way to merely draw shapes in someone's back yard hoping someone would notice?
Steve Kenney, USA

Years ago in Minnesota, a UFO believer had a joke played on him by his brother-in-law. The in-law made circular burn marks in the man's cornfield. The UFO believer was ecstatic to find the discovery on his property. A few days later, the joker in law informed him it was a gag that he went to a great deal of trouble to play on him. No matter. The UFO believer still thought he had alien visitors. They are a stubborn breed, those UFO freaks.
David Hulbert, USA

The only reasonable argument for crop circles being of 'alien' construction would be that they only seem to appear in localised areas of the world in arable farmland. This, however is also the most convincing argument against the 'alien' theories, I mean, who has ever heard of a mud circle or a dust circle? This is either the work of intelligent life-forms, or people from Hampshire.
Lisa Harvey-Smith, England

So little green men are flying billions of miles in highly sophisticated craft simply in order to hide behind clouds and draw circles in cornfields near where hippies are squatting? Hmm ... maybe not.
Gretl Coudrille, UK

Maybe, maybe not there is no solid proof either way.
Efrem Gebrehiwet, Canada

Aliens? No. A Hoax? No. Natural phenomenon? Quite plausible. There are many things we don't yet understand about this sphere we live on. The corn lays undamaged facing the same way with no footprints approaching the patterns. I doubt a hoaxer would be able to create this effect with string and a plank of wood without damaging the crop. This study should include a timed attempt at creating these intricate circles using sting and planks of wood, and see if they can achieve the same effect.
Michael, UK

Since these formations are only properly visible from the air, isn't it obvious that it's not passing aliens signalling to us, but aliens here on earth sending messages to their airborne brethren ? By a stroke of luck, the peak foreign holiday season on Mars coincides with the best growing season in Wiltshire.
Dave Smith, UK

Fake? What do you think? I can just imagine...somewhere on the far side of the galaxy a race of aliens have spent vital resources and years building a craft, and training their crew. Then travel in suspended animation and suffer the perils of deep space, potential super novae, black holes and worse, arrive on earth, 'draw' pretty diagrams amongst plants - crop circles - and then, without a word head back home. Mission accomplished. This is millennial madness, and sadly the result of a post-Christian society looking to the sky for a God-substitute.
Jon Gardner, England

Wouldn't it just be the most amazing thing to happen to us, if there was something out there coming to visit us.
Shabaz Siddique, England

Clearly not many of these respondents have actually been in a crop formation nor have they sought any information other than that which is presented to them. Why do cameras and mobile phones fail to operate in formations? Why do dogs often refuse to enter? Why have some post-menopausal women started bleeding again? Why do many people report dizziness and nausea, others elation

and peace? Why does lodging (aka. wind damage) show similar physical effects to those found in crops circles? Where are the photographs of hoaxers in mid-creation? Why haven't any been caught and prosecuted?
Damian Brothers, England

It is a sad reflection on mankind as we approach the new millennium that superstition and irrationality still guide the thought processes of so many people.
Richard Gibson, UK

Unexplained phenomenon are always a challenge to any people. Crop circles are not recent, but ancient, and clearly challenge explanation. No so-called hoaxers could do this. Let's hope the research scheduled this year will bring some new facts out!
Robert Heilman, USA

Of course they are fake. They are planted just like the cereal they are made in. How come few are caught doing it? Imagine: Helicopter dangling disc at end of a line. The spinning disc causes the effect of a circle in the crop. Helicopter goes away. Crop circle formed by "mysterious" craft!
Graham Roberts, UK

Just ask yourself one question, why would a species intelligent enough to cross vast distances of empty space land on a planet and make pretty circles in the fields of crops? Crop circles have always been the work of terrestrial beings armed with string, ladders, planks and sense of humour.
Ian Thomas, England

I believe they are a craze just as is graffiti.
Michael Smith, UK

I have seen many crop circles as I used to live in the Marlborough Downs where great many of the crop circles appeared in the early nineties. I can honestly say that the locals including the farmers are just as puzzled as everyone else. The things I remember are the fact the corn is not broken but bent over and still alive. Some of the crop circles were impossible to get to. Strange electromagnetic fields seem to be around some the crop circles and I remember TV

cameramen not being able to film the crop circles close up due to malfunctioning cameras.
Tim, England

Of course they're a hoax. It may be absurd to suggest we're the only intelligent life in the universe, but it's just as ludicrous to think that aliens would travel for centuries, millennia even, purely to mess around in our farms. Besides, I know someone who does it. Although his are frankly rubbish. But then, I'm not sure he isn't an alien anyhow.

Rob Marriott, UK

In my opinion crop circles are not a hoax, I base my theory on the fact that some of the circles that have been produced overnight both in the U.K and abroad are far too intricate in design to have been knocked up by someone with a torch and a lawn mower. At the end of the day I personally feel that people are experiencing a classic fear of the unknown and dealing with this by labelling these and other strange phenomena as the work of hoaxers when really they don't have a clue and this is the most convenient answer.
P.Fletcher, England

Of course they're a hoax - the hoaxers have put their hands up! The persistence of this kind of new age thinking in the face of all the evidence including the confessions of those responsible is more worthy of research than are crop circles.
Paul Cooper, UK

How about putting one in for the Turner prize? There's no doubt they are of human origin and it's no more dotty that wearing strange hats crossing London Bridge last May 'for art'.
K. Jackson, USA

Judging from the amount and frequency of these 'phenomena' I believe it seems rather too much like hard work to be a hoax. But to suggest the involvement of extra-terrestrial life is far-fetched. This money would be better spent investigating whether Scottish football referees are in fact aliens.
Gus McGhee, Germany

It would be rather depressing to think that after the vast expense and time it would take to reach our planet that all the 'visitors' wished to do was vandalise a few crops!! Plus, how come we don't get similar patterns appearing on snow?
John Wedderburn, UK

When crops are given too much fertiliser, they become too top heavy and are easily blown over by the wind. If you were to add fertiliser to the ground before planting in a 'crop circle' pattern, when it grows the pattern will emerge as the areas of fallen crops.
Colin Harrison, UK

Hoax? No way! Even on the picture on the top of this page you can see that they are real and created with techniques we have absolutely no idea of. Besides all of these marks have meanings. This one shows Earth and Moon. Earth is the third planet from the sun and we can see that Earth symbol is marked with 3 vertical lines aside. Moon is the only Earth's satellite and we can see that Moon sign is marked with 1 vertical line. Besides, Earth and Moon proportions showed by these signs match real ones. It's a disputable question who creates these marks. But one can be said for sure: no one on Earth can do this so precisely.
Alex Wierzbowsky, EU

There are no aliens and there are no UFO's and all this is just a hoax. (what most people who believe in UFO's do not realise that even if there were space travellers, they could not get here as they would be too far away to find us.)
And also probably we are the only intelligent life form anywhere in the universe. Even it there is life of any kind in our galaxy, or any galaxy, it is so far away, that we are never going to find it, or know about it. Yes, we are alone!!!
Marius Balogh, Australia

They're either a hoax of an earthly nature or there are some very bored ET's out there having a joke at our expense!
Guy Dawson, UK

The whole 'crop circles are formed by aliens' malarkey is a swizz. Quite honestly, I think people believing in extra-terrestrial activity

in cornfields are quite mad. Wheat, fields on the other hand...
Rupert C Kent, London, UK

Crop circles definitely exist. My garden backs onto a large field of barley. One morning, many many moons ago I awoke to find the local farmer scratching his head and chewing his corn in a very perplexed manner. When I enquired as to his confusion he told me to go upstairs and gaze over his field. I did this and low and behold there was a perfect circle of flattened barley in the middle of the field.
Naturally I expected tom foolery from the local ruffians but when he pointed out that there were marks leading into the field, I had to scratch my head in amazement too. There had been many strange goings on in the hamlet round then, only that night had a large helicopter landed in the field!!!
Michael Norton, England

Of course Corn Circles are fake! But that is not the issue - the issue is why do so many people believe that aliens could be responsible? It appears to me that these people believe in a whole load of twaddle - all this 'New Age' nonsense - probably something to do with the breakdown of ordered religion for many people in this country - they're searching for some spiritual fulfilment. Well, they won't find it in a field full if hippies off the M4!
They need a cold shower!
Charles Ungard, UK

Although some corn-circles are certainly hoaxes, the sites that are confirmed as being made by humans tend to be rather simplistic, tatty affairs, quite unlike the geometric precision and beauty found in some examples. There is no way that these are produced by hoaxers.
I don't believe aliens have anything to do with it either and I personally support the freak weather conditions or natural phenomenon explanations but I hope that this new study can provide some definite proof.
Dave Cogbill, UK

Either a hoax or demonic activity!
E.W. Dunn UK

There is no hoax. Nor is there any indication that they are anything other than natural phenomena.
Daryle Denomy, Canada

So we get crop circles but no desert circles, forest circles, pasture circles, pebble circles - I would expect the superior beings who are our alleged visitors to do something a little more impressive than flatten down a bit of corn.
Maybe they just wanted to freak out the farmers, or perhaps writing any of the extremely basic languages used to communicate on this planet is beyond them??
Long may crop circles continue if it means more Yankee dollars coming our way!
Richard, UK

The public seem to be very misinformed about crop circles in general. The BBC Country File program did nothing that wasn't already known about the phenomenon. What they failed to show after the circles had been made was the broken stems that were strewn over all the formations, something that is not seen in many of the others.
Crop circle investigators have been asked to prove that they are genuine. The so-called "crop circle artists", "hoaxers", etc have never been asked to provide evidence of which formations they have made. Based on this I can claim to have made every circle in the world.
As for Laurance Rockefeller funding research. Who are his scientists? Where are they from? There is a lack of basic investigation from croppies and media alike.
Mark Haywood UK

High numbers of Young Farmers equals high numbers of crop circles, I think there is a connection.
M. Gallacher, Scotland

Hmm... If those circles were a hoax, then how come their creators have not been caught on a single occasion, in a relatively dense populated island, such as Britain?
I believe that human mind alone cannot be so creative... until it's exposed to AN EXAMPLE, and then just modifies it and simulates. My opinion, reasoning from the info I got so far, those

circles are indeed something of "outer" nature.
Alex "Sasha", Russia

Since the men responsible for the whole hoax have already come
forward and flawlessly reproduced the crop circles, this seems like
a moot point. But then people generally don't like their beliefs
questioned, so I'm not surprised that the debate still lingers.
Croppists are looking for ways to explain an existing belief; they
should instead be looking at beliefs to explain existing facts. But
how often does that happen?
Kat, USA

Perhaps crop circles are the work of inter-galactic graffiti artists.
Translated they probably say 'Zog Was Here'.
Phil Huddlestone, UK

The most noticeable thing about the current wave of crop circles is
how close many of them are to tourist sites like Avebury and
Glastonbury - just what you need to get a good hoax noticed!
Of course, the New Agers claim this is due to the 'mystical power'
of such sites, but I prefer the simpler explanation that people like
their work to get attention.
James W Bottomley, UK

A few friends and myself created a circle one night. The resulting
investigation by UFO "experts" showed strange radiation readings
and psychic vibes in the centre of the circle. It just shows how
stupid some people are.
Joe, England

Has anyone ever been caught making a crop formation? No.
Wiltshire is not the back of beyond. Whilst there is no doubt that
many formations, in this country at least are manmade, this does
not explain the 10,000 plus formations that have appeared in India
in the last twenty years, many of them in remote fields far away
from media cameras and tourists.
Neill Wood, UK

How many of the hoaxers must confess before it is accepted that
they are a hoax? Why do so many people insist that there be proof
that flying saucers don't exist? Accept the evidence (the

confessions) and let the rest of us get on with our lives.
Richard T. Ketchum, USA

While I generally approve of seriously-minded scientific investigation of unexplained phenomena - after all, lightning bolts were supposed to be all sorts of paranormal things until Benjamin Franklin put his mind to work - I can't help feeling that crop circles hold no great discovery for mankind. Except, perhaps, that some forms of graffiti are much more imaginative than others.
M. Reed Austin, UK

I am a tax advisor and drink shandy. Only when me and my advisor chums have had too little lemonade in our shandies and get a little boisterous do we go out and try and make crop circles. Unfortunately they are usually crop squiggles.
Steve McMullen, England

Hasn't anyone else noticed that the first link site is by the circle makers themselves?
David, UK

Hail fellow Kights! Crop circles are the work of my teams of Pixie Knights in their relentless pursuit of Pixie Magic.
King Arthur of Camalot, England

Crop Circles are by far the most interesting mystery of the 20th century. We have more or less successfully debunked Nessie and Bigfoot and all that rubbish, crop circles are still, unexplained for the most part.
They happen in too many places, too often, for even a fairly well organised group of persons would be hard pressed not to EVER get caught.
Crop Circles are scary, they are unknown, that is why most of the people here are moved to write, and to assert they 'do not exist'.
Roger, USA

I am 74 years old and can remember crop circles in cornfields from when I was a child living first in Norfolk and later in Dorset. Some of them were quite elaborate. The country people accepted them, they were part of the landscape, and had been for generations.
There was no talk of them being hoaxed in those days, people were

much more law abiding, and the thought of deliberately damaging a farmer's crop was unthinkable.
I have always believed a proportion of the formations are real.
Sam Dalston, UK

Anybody who takes a step back to consider this 'phenomenon' realises that aliens, or any other alternative explanation just does not hold up. Even a die hard believer forced to answer why the aliens have targeted corn fields of all places, and why these bizarre patterns have been the result of technology far beyond us usually concedes the point.
Other forms of intelligence are very likely to exist - but get real. Corn circles have nothing whatsoever to do with that issue.
Chafir, England

I've seen a few circles from the air myself. All were connected to a road or track, either by tractor ruts or a direct path in the crops in some cases! Is this proof that aliens walk?
The real mystery is why people prefer to believe their own fantasies, rather than testimony and demonstrations from the hoaxers.
Then again, some people believe that Eastenders is a fly-on-the-wall documentary!
Rik Alewijnse, UK

Crop circle tours are selling out? A US billionaire is financing an investigation? Sounds like a money maker to me.
Tim Donovan, US

Printed in Great Britain
by Amazon

43894063R00076